Cobweb Helps a Friend

Written by Daphne Faunce-Brown
Illustrated by Lynne Byrnes

For the Craigmore hedgehogs

COBWEB is a bright-eyed, prickly hedgehog who lives next door to a long, brown centipede.

Cobweb and Wellington — that's the centipede's name — are close friends.

Unfortunately, Wellington has a serious problem. Like all centipedes, he has one hundred legs and, as he hates to have wet feet, he wears fifty pairs of wellington boots to keep his feet dry! He often has to buy new pairs and he can never remember which pair should fit which feet.

One very wet day, when Wellington had so many blisters from wearing his boots on the wrong feet that his toes were covered in sticking plasters, he had an idea.

"I know," he thought, "I'll tie my boots together in fifty pairs." He fetched some string from the kitchen and spent the rest of that day sorting out his boots into pairs and tying them together.

Wellington felt rather proud of himself as he arranged his fifty pairs of boots in a long and tidy line outside his front door, ready for the morning.

He went happily to bed and slept well.

Later that night, Cobweb noticed the row of wellington boots and laughed mischievously to himself.

It would be fun, he thought, to mix them up and to cross some of the strings over each other.

That is exactly what he did.

You should have seen Wellington in the morning!

He pulled on his boots in no time at all, but when he tried to walk, he could hardly move. He got into a terrible muddle. Some boots were too tight and others fell off because they were too loose. He fell over some of the strings and was very angry.

"Someone has got a funny sense of humour," he muttered, as he stamped into his house, leaving his boots in an untidy heap.

Cobweb was watching all of this from a safe distance, and laughed until he cried.

However, he was a good-natured hedgehog and very fond of Wellington and he felt he had been rather unkind.

Cobweb wanted to help. He thought about Wellington's problem for a long time and then he fetched his tins of paint and his brushes.

He carefully sorted the one hundred boots into fifty pairs. Then he painted ten pairs black, ten pairs green, ten pairs yellow, ten pairs blue but he left the last ten pairs red.

This would certainly help his friend.

1
2
3
4
5

However, to make things even easier for Wellington, Cobweb took a tin of white paint and numbered each set of colours. He painted 1, 2, 3, 4, 5, 6, 7, 8, 9, 10 on all of the left boots of each colour and then did the same to the right boots.

Cobweb felt very pleased with himself as he put his paints and brushes away.

Wellington was delighted when he saw the row of colourful boots in the morning. He knew that Cobweb must have painted them for him, as no other friend could count as far as ten!

He thanked Cobweb again and again. The two friends laughed about the string and agreed that this was a far better idea.

10
9
8
7
6
5
4

If you ever see a brown centipede wearing red, blue, yellow, green and black wellington boots and they are numbered 1, 2, 3, 4, 5, 6, 7, 8, 9, 10, you will know that it is Wellington.

4 5 6 7 8 9 10
1 2 3 4 5 6 7 8 9 10
1 2 3 4 5 6 7 8 9 10

You may see Cobweb with Wellington, as Wellington needs new boots every now and then and Cobweb always paints them for him.

Published by
Studio Publications (Ipswich) Limited
32 Princes Street, Ipswich IP1 1RJ

Printed and bound in Great Britain